These Words That Fail Me

Tanner S. Soles

BookLeaf Publishing

Presentation by *BookLeaf Publishing*

Web: www.bookleafpub.com

E-mail: info@bookleafpub.com

ISBN: 9789357448529

First edition 2022

For Mum; thank you for supporting my writing
endeavours from the beginning

and

For Bolder; even though you couldn't care less
about poetry and art, you have always been my
Muse

Birth

1

The squeezing is gone,
Then cold, bright first breath of air.
Eyes open, meet mum.

For My Oldest Child

The night after you were born, I lay awake,
Still choking on awe, counting every breath
Fearful each might be the last you would take
Like a fragile chick, too soon to meet death

The night you were born, my heart tore in two
Not broken, but burst, having been too small
Too small to hold infinite love for you

For you I'd build the world up from bare groun'
And for you, I would burn the whole thing down

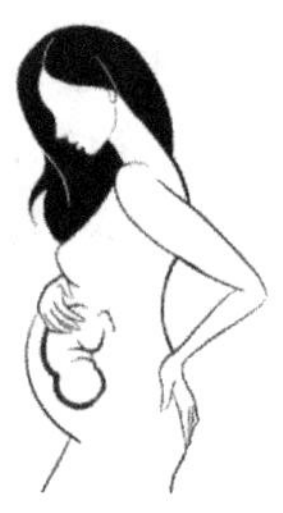

For My Second Child

5

When I grew wide with your tiny body
I feared I'd love you less than your brother
How could I possibly love another,
When he already was the world to me?
Then you entered this mad, crazy world,
And I saw I had no need to worry,
As wide as the sky my heart unfurled.

The river flowing through the deep canyon
Isn't less than the one with which it began
Somehow you both can be my only one
And will be as long as my life will span.

Being Mother

Sometimes, being a mother
Is trying not to laugh
As your child smears banana on their legs,
Or tries to tuck a piece of liquorice between your
toes,
Then having to figure out how to tell them
That is not something people do

For my Mum

9

From when merely walking was still my highest
aim
You taught me most everything, taught me how
to learn
Through struggles, absurd and true, you were
there the same

Now I'm a woman, you still answer every call.
You are now both beloved mum and friend most
true.
My highest, my lowest, you've loved me
through it all.

Before the comfort of home, or thrill of
something new
Before I knew the sky, before I knew my name
Before that, and further, I've known that I love
you

Fortieth Birthday Poem For My Mum

So, it's your birthday. I understand
That you're turning 40, isn't that grand?
Some get upset because they feel old
But the older the wiser, is what I've been told
So, don't get depressed
And don't be stressed
You're still the same woman you'll always be
And you're never too old to live happily

For My Husband

Some days your practicality is painfully extreme
And I wish for adventure and excitement
Or to go together to do something you would
deem
A waste of time or unimportant

But then I call to mind the little things I love
about you
And I remember that I also love your practical
ways
The little day to day things you do
I love you on the level of every days

When you bring me my morning coffee,
When going out means looking at real-estate,
When you read our babies a bedtime story,
When you take over a chore that I hate.

Flaws and strengths, both one and the same
So to balance each other should be our aim

Opening Up

The key falls from the lock
But the soul knows not what it means
Not yet
It still peers through the bars,
The cage, the cold chest.

Gryphon looks on with patience
Certain,
So certain,
Too certain,
That it is for the best.
Despite the burning evidence all around him
Against it.

Cold and calculating, she feels that key,
To her heart, her soul, her inner workings,
And for once, thoughts do not hold the answer
She has broken her every rule
Letting him get this close.
Fear,
Excitement,
Disbelief,
And maybe
Just maybe
A spark of hope,
Rage through her.

But mostly fear.
Her face holds no hint of it.
It consumes her.

All around,
The world watches on.
In sweet oblivion to cold truth,
To impending fire.
So beautiful
So foolish
So doomed
Perhaps that is why,
With all seemingly so hopeless,
She has allowed this opening.
If all is in vain,
Why try to preserve her sanity?
Or insanity?
Or anything?

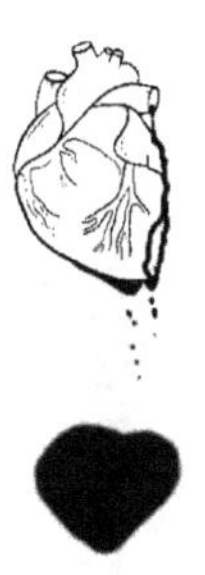

love poem 1

Grief, I have heard people tell
Is love with nowhere to go
I like this explanation well
Because that's how I feel you know

I can hear your voice across the phone
But this pain still fills my heart
You are so far away, I feel so alone
How can we keep what is bound so close so far
apart?

My love is caged within my chest
But it longs to search and find you
I doubt that I will truly rest
Until I can do so beside you

How can a feeling run so strong?
It's mixed with the blood in my veins.
It has been for so long
That hardly a memory of before remains.

How much I love you I cannot express
And oh, how I wish to
I believe it will only pain me less
Once I can fully express it to you.

Confession

When I told you,
the fear almost clogged my throat.
 I couldn't stand to see the disgust in those blue
eyes.
I fixed my eyes on the corner where the wall and
the ceiling met.

It tumbled out of my gut like a flood,
lapping at the darkness around our bed
Turning it from churning soot into ink.
At least it was no longer in my lungs.

When I was done, I lay there in silence.
Not knowing what would happen next…
it gaped at me, as vast as the universe.
I feared being lost out in that expanse.

Then ever-loving arms wrapped around me
you drew me out of that ocean of guilt

Winter

22

Winter is when God looks down and says "these
silly people don't know how to rest."
So, he makes it so that they cannot do much
else.
He pears down the colors to black and white
and lets time freeze up a little.
He gives us little things
that promote rest.
A fire to
curl up beside,
Warm comfort foods,
Starry night skies
dancing with lights.

Maybe one day
we'll remember
that even God
rested on the
seventh day

First Frost

24

Frosted grass on path
Underneath my heavy boot
Frozen mud crunches

The Wicklefree

26

the Wicklefree is stomping about
he is mad there is no doubt
but there is no need to worry
for we have a Tickelry
so as long as he keeps out his snout
we can keep on going about

Flight

28

Flying
Silver wings
Cut the sky
Beneath them
Earth stretches
Meeting sky.
Horizon.
Misty haze.

A cloud bank
High above
We meet it
Like a wave.
Water flow
In the sky
Moist kiss
Of vapor.
Then we break
Out above
The rolling,
Churning sea.

Beside us
Burns heaven's
Flaming orb
A stone's throw

Away from
Our wing's tip.

It seems like
We are out
Of time's reach
I can see
Everything
Yet nothing
Is too big.
Perspective.

We start decent
And then reality
Rushes back up to meet us
And the world closes up around us once again

The Curse of the Chicken Tomb

31

Doom will zoom
 to bloom
  and loom
   in him whom
    eats chicken plume
     from this tomb

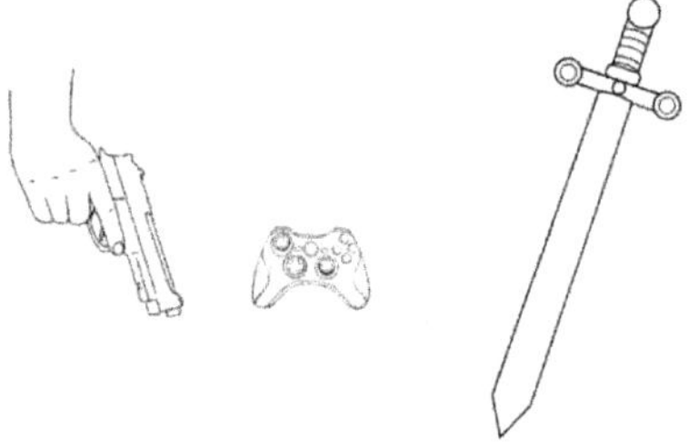

Colosseum

Roaring crowds
All around
Dry ground,
Soon to be
Wet with red
Scent of fear
Drown beneath
Our bloodlust
Fight begins
Stab, perry, slash
To the throat
To the side
To the knee
Pain
Pain
Pain
And he falls
And we roar
We want blood
We get it
Skip ahead
Silver screen
The battle
Rages on
My eyes watch
Hungering

For the scene
Warrior falls
To cold mud
Above him
A face looms
Can't look away
Can't help it
Gun comes up
Bang
Bang
Bang
Screen goes dark
Skip ahead
Pixel gun
No blood scent
No soreness
No pain
No anything
All the thrill
Is long gone
This last kill
All alone
In my room
On the screen
And this game
Isn't enough
Anymore
Skip ahead

You're Damned if You Do

"The love of new knowledge is dangerous
The way that it can sway your very mind,
The way that it can make your morals rust
The way that it can cause you to go blind"

"A good speaker's words can easily sway
both a person's mind and a person's heart
To the point you wake up and find one day
You cannot tell your thoughts and theirs apart"

"You must be careful to only read
That with which you can already agree
In case it sews in you a tiny seed
After all, who knows what its fruit may be?"

Does knowledge really breed belligerence?
Perhaps it's all this wilful ignorance.

and You're Damned If You Don't

"The latest great thing is always best,
You must follow each new theory and whim
You cannot put anything to the test,
You do not know enough to question them."

"Do not question what 'experts' say is true,
They say it's logical? Then it must be!
Don't you know they know far more than you
do?
If you ask for proof you're just a dummy"

"You must agree with every point of view
Or else you are just being close-minded
If you trust in the old things that you knew
Then you are simply being short sighted"

Is the newest thing always the best to do?
What ever happened to what's tried and true?